LONDON'S RAILWAYS SINCE THE 1970S

JOHN LAW

AMBERLEY

First published 2021

Amberley Publishing
The Hill, Stroud
Gloucestershire, GL5 4EP

www.amberley-books.com

Copyright © John Law, 2021

The right of John Law to be identified as
the Author of this work has been asserted in
accordance with the Copyrights, Designs and
Patents Act 1988.

ISBN 978 1 4456 9573 0 (print)
ISBN 978 1 4456 9574 7 (ebook)

British Library Cataloguing in Publication Data.
A catalogue record for this book is available from
the British Library.

Origination by Amberley Publishing.
Printed in the UK.

Introduction

What is now the County of Greater London was formed in 1965 and made the boundaries of the area covered by this publication. The author moved to London in 1970 and has lived there or close by for fifty years, thirty-five of which were spent in the employ of British Rail and its successors.

In 1970, London's railways were undergoing great changes. Everything was being painted in corporate blue, steam traction in the area had ceased three years earlier and a BR locomotive renumbering scheme was about to take place.

Perhaps it is best to look at each group of lines individually, to enable the changes to be examined over the course of the last fifty years. Travelling round London in an anti-clockwise direction, we start with the former London, Tilbury and Southend Railway, from its main terminus in the City, Fenchurch Street. Dubbed the 'Misery Line' by the local media, the route suffered from outdated infrastructure and rolling stock until thoroughly modernised around the turn of the century. Having had a spell under the auspices of National Express (who called it 'C2C'), the franchise was later sold to Trenitalia.

Great changes are coming to the former Great Eastern lines as these lines are being penned. Greater Anglia, a joint venture between Nederlandse Spoorwegen and a Japanese company called Mitsui & Co., trading as Abellio, are running services into Cambridgeshire, Essex and beyond. Meanwhile TfL Rail will eventually be operating the Elizabeth Line (formerly known as Crossrail), now expected to open in 2022. In addition, London Overground has taken over the suburban services up the Lea Valley.

London Overground is also now operating orbital services on the North London Line with modern rolling stock. Once running from Broad Street to Richmond, this was very much a forgotten backwater of British Rail. Previously diesel operated, the Gospel Oak to Barking has recently been electrified and is even being extended to a new development at Barking Riverside.

Another former backwater, the West London Line from Willesden to Clapham Junction, has also been upgraded and now sees regular electric services operated by London Overground and Southern.

The London Underground has seen major improvements since 1970, starting with the completion of the Victoria Line. Another development was that of the Jubilee Line, now serving the once derelict former dockland area. Perhaps the major improvement around the East End has been the building of the Docklands Light Railway, which now serves parts of South East London too.

The 1970s saw the Great Northern route out of Kings Cross receive 25kv overhead catenary, with the third rail DC being installed on the ex-London Underground 'Northern City' route to Moorgate. Kings Cross station has recently undergone a major reconstruction, retaining many of its original featured. Many of the outer suburban and local services are now diverted along a new subterranean connection and now serve the Thameslink routes via St Pancras. That station, the Midland Railway's London terminal, has seen major changes. The station is now divided into four separate sectors, with both Eurostar and Southeastern services diverging onto the new High Speed line via Stratford International.

Euston station had recently been rebuilt by 1970 and its rail services electrified. Otherwise little had changed from the days of steam. Pendolino sets, fitted with tilt technology, now dominate the Intercity routes, while modern EMUs have replaced the original 501 and 310 units previously used on local services.

One of the success stories of privatisation is Chiltern Railways, who took over the services out of Marylebone. This station has gone from a run-down location that served only DMUs to Aylesbury and High Wycombe (some ran a bit further via Bicester), to today's modern trains to Birmingham and Oxford. Yet it came so close to complete closure!

Paddington, Brunel's GWR London terminus, is still the gateway to the West of England. Electrification came in 1998, just out to Hayes and Harlington and the brand new branch to Heathrow Airport. Today, most of the GWR route is under 25kv catenary, with new IEP trains operating the Intercity services. Diesel units are still employed on the West Ealing to Greenford branch. Class 345 Aventra EMUs are already in use on Paddington to Reading stopping services and when the Elizabeth line finally opens, they will take over through the central core. They will be based at the new depot on the former Old Oak Common depot site.

Taking the Southern Region as a whole, it was, until the 1980s, the bastion of slam-door rolling stock. Gradually the SUB and EPB types have been replaced with a variety of EMUs. Surprisingly perhaps, there have been a few line closures, including Elmers End to Selsdon and Addiscombe, plus Wimbledon to West Croydon. These services have been replaced in the most part by those of Croydon Tramlink, using the trackbed in some cases.

The Southern's major Central London stations have been modernised, with Charing Cross, Cannon Street and the 'Brighton' side of Victoria being covered over by commercial development. Waterloo saw a new section built to handle Eurostar services, only for it to revert to domestic use after trains for the Continent were rerouted into St Pancras. Holborn Viaduct station has vanished, while Blackfriars has undergone a complete rebuild, all part of the 'Thameslink 2000' project. Perhaps the biggest transformation, though, is that of London Bridge, truly a twenty-first-century station.

The future for London's railways looks bright. The Elizabeth Line looks set to open in 2022. HS2, the new high-speed railway to the north, is under construction, starting from its projected terminal at Euston and calling at a new interchange facility at Old Oak Common. That will undoubtedly change the pattern of journeys in the capital. Let us look forward to it all.

Finally, it should be noted that many of the photographs in this book were taken during the course of the author's thirty-five years employment in the railway industry, with appropriate safety measures in place as necessary. The author does not condone trespassing on railway property.

The author is grateful to the following for supplying a few photographs: Richard Huggins, Alan James, Kevin Lane, Hugh Llewelyn and the Late Tony Martens.

London, Tilbury and Southend Lines

Back in 1971 the mainstay of London, Tilbury and Southend (LT&S) line services were operated by electrical multiple units (EMUs) built in the late 1950s/early 1960s. Later to be known as Class 302, unit No. 268 is seen arriving at its London terminus, Fenchurch Street. The driver has already set the destination for its next working.

The Class 305 EMU was intended for inner suburban services out of London Liverpool Street to Enfield and Hertford East. By the time of this photograph, spring 1991, unit 305 503 had transferred to the LT&S line. It is pictured awaiting departure in the bay platform at Upminster, forming the shuttle service to Grays.

Much of the LT&S section was controlled by small signal boxes such as this one at Dagenham Dock, on the Tilbury Loop. As well as supervising the level crossing, it also controlled access into Ford's extensive sidings. The photograph was taken in December 1993, not long before Upminster Integrated Electronic Control Centre replaced it.

Today's LT&S services are operated by c2c (now part of Trenitalia). Most services are operated using air-conditioned EMUs such as 357 204, seen arriving at Rainham station, on the very edge of Greater London, on 1 July 2014

Great Eastern Lines

The Great Eastern Railway's main London terminus was the vast station known as Liverpool Street. In the early 1970s, EMUs were in charge of both inner and outer suburban services, but diesel locomotives were used to haul express trains to the likes of Cambridge and Norwich. Railway enthusiasts would often visit the locomotive stabling point by the country end of the platforms and here, in 1971, Brush type 2 No. 5512 was photographed. Built in 1957 as part of the pilot scheme preceding the main batch, it was later renumbered 31 012.

For many years, Liverpool Street was home to a 'station pilot', a small locomotive used for shunting parcels vans, etc. In steam days it would have been a J69 0-6-0T, but by the mid-1970s a Stratford-based 350hp diesel was used. Here we have 08 752 resting between duties, while the rake of Mark 2 carriages seen behind it will form an InterCity service.

Liverpool Street suburban services out to Gidea Park and Shenfield were in the hands of LNER designed three-car EMUs fitted with sliding doors. Originally operating on 1,500 DC power, they were later converted to AC and became BR's Class 306. In 1976 unit 018 was photographed arriving at Stratford on an up working. Cross-platform interchange with the Underground's Central Line was possible here. The majority of the 306 units were withdrawn in the early 1980s.

In the 1970s the majority of InterCity services did not call at Stratford. Passing through the station on an up Norwich service formed of Mark I stock is 37 033, *c*. 1975. Stratford's power signal box can be seen to the left of the locomotive, with the little used (then) Lea Valley platforms beyond.

Back at Liverpool Street, sometime around 1978. It is here that we see Brush Type 4 No. 47 018, ready to leave with an InterCity service. Built as early as 1964, when it was known as D1572, it is obviously a Stratford-based engine – the silver roof gives that away. It remained at Stratford until 1982 and finally succumbed to the breaker's torch in 1994.

British Rail began introducing the Class 312 type EMU from 1975. It transpired that they were to be the last units to employ the Mark 2 coach body shell and the last sets to be built with slam doors. The class was divided into three: the 312/0 units going to the Great Northern line, a few 312/3 were built for the West Midlands, and the 312/1 sets going to the Great Eastern. The latter were originally painted in all-over blue, as seen applied to 312 112 at Liverpool Street forming a semi-fast Colchester service in 1976.

In the 1970s, British Rail was using Class 305 EMUs on local services up the Lea Valley from Liverpool Street to destinations like Enfield Town and Hertford East. Here, three-car set 448 calls at Clapton in the mid-1970s. Construction of the 305 units began in 1959 and the final ones were withdrawn in 2001.

The Class 315 EMUs were the last of a long line of similar trains that were introduced during the 1970s for the Southern Region, the Great Northern, Merseyside and Glasgow. Construction of the 315 sets began in York in 1980, these being for AC overhead power only. Newly delivered in blue and grey, set 315 826 awaits departure for Shenfield (all stations) at Liverpool Street in 1981.

Stratford was the main works and repair facility for the former Great Eastern lines. Gradually a lot of the buildings became unused but the Traction Maintenance Depot (TMD) survived into the twenty-first century. In mid-1979 the depot was home to a pair of BR built Class 03 shunters: 03 081 and 03 047. 081 lives on in preservation at Mangapps Farm.

British Rail commenced construction of the Class 58 diesel freight locomotives at Doncaster in 1982. The second one built, 58 002, is seen at Stratford TMD on 9 July 1983 in its grey 'Railfreight' livery. Like most of the class, it did not have a long life and was withdrawn in 2000.

Some residual freight traffic survived within the 'teardrop' of railways forming the boundaries of the Stratford area, close to High Meads Junction, where the resident shunter, 08 393, was photographed in early 2000. This loco later received EWS red livery, but has since been withdrawn. The whole area was later cleared and became the site of Stratford International station, the 2012 Olympic site and the Westgate Shopping Centre.

In the 1970s an infrequent and little-used service ran between Tottenham Hale and North Woolwich via Stratford Low Level. It was operated by DMUs, such as this Cravens Class 105 set, seen calling at a virtually derelict Lea Bridge station on 10 May 1985, only two months before the station closed to passengers. However, recent developments in the area have seen the reopening of the station with an enhanced timetable.

In the early 1970s, London's docklands had just about ceased commercial activity. The diesel-operated North Woolwich branch passed through the area. In 1971, some of the disused sidings serving the port facilities can be seen on the right of Custom House station, as a BRCW DMU departs for its riverside terminus.

The terminus at North Woolwich had, by the mid-1970s, become a single platform affair, more than adequate to serve the DMU service. Here, a Class 105 set has just arrived and the driver is about to change the destination blind for its return to Stratford or Tottenham Hale. The station buildings at North Woolwich later became a museum, but this has since closed. The Docklands Light Railway now operates rail services in the area.

Another DMU service in East London in the 1970s was that between Romford and Upminster. Though the line was built by the London, Tilbury & Southend Railway, the physical connection at the LT&S end was severed many years ago and Stratford-based units serviced the line. Here, in 1971, a three-car set (incorrectly displaying 'Broxbourne' as its destination) arrives at the only intermediate station – Emerson Park.

Since 1986, the Romford to Upminster service has been electrified, though still operated as a self-contained shuttle service. In the spring of 1991, Network SouthEast liveried EMU 315 817 was in use and was photographed in its own platform at Romford station.

The Great Eastern Railway built the suburban line to Chingford with the intention of carrying on further into Essex, reflecting on the design of today's terminus. In 1976 the service to Liverpool Street was operated by Class 305 EMUs, four of which are visible in this view.

The date is 11 July 2007 and National Express (trading as 'One') has the franchise for the Great Eastern routes, including Chingford. Here, 315 818 rests in what was intended to be one of the through platforms. At the time of writing the Class 315 EMUs are being withdrawn and scrapped.

The Network SouthEast sector of British Rail ordered a large batch of Class 321 EMUs, the first being delivered in 1988 for former GER line services. Probably heading for Southend Victoria, unit 321 353 departs from Romford in spring 1991. At the time of writing, Greater Anglia operates the entire fleet of 321 units, mainly on outer suburban duties.

Though the inner and outer suburban former GER lines had long been electrified, it was not until in 1987 that the InterCity route to Norwich received 25kv overhead wires. A number of Class 86 electric locomotives were transferred from the London Midland Region. These were later painted into privatised colours, as seen on 86 215 by the buffer stops at Liverpool Street in summer 1999. The Class 86 locos were later replaced by 90s that, in turn, succumbed to new EMU types.

Freight traffic at the terminal at Bow, between Stratford and Liverpool Street, increased markedly during the construction of the Olympic site. The Dockland Light Railway platforms of Pudding Mill Lane provided a grandstand panorama of the operations. From that viewpoint we see Freightliner 66 604 on a loaded aggregate service on 21 August 2009.

For future Crossrail services a large batch of Class 345 Aventra EMUs was ordered from Bombardier Transportation. Delays in the opening of the central tunnel section of Crossrail (now known as the Elizabeth Line) meant that the new units took over some services out of Paddington, plus the frequent Liverpool Street to Shenfield all stations route. At the time of writing, the Elizabeth Line is expected to open in 2022, having been further put back by the Covid-19 pandemic of 2020. Here, on 30 June 2017, unit 345 007 departs eastwards out of Romford.

London's Orbital Routes

In this section we look at the North London Line, which connected at Gospel Oak with the line to Barking. It also had a junction with the West London Line through Kensington Olympia. Until 1986, what was effectively a branch, albeit a four-track one, ran from Dalston Junction on the North London route to a city terminus at Broad Street. It is, therefore, appropriate that it is included in this section. Broad Street station in the 1970s was very run down, with just the service to Richmond and peak-hour-only trains to Watford and the Great Northern line. In this 1976 view a Class 501 EMU is berthed in the station, as the National Westminster Tower is under construction.

The Class 501 units, built in the mid-1950s, were the mainstay of services into Broad Street, but trains heading for the unelectrified Great Northern lines were formed of DMUs. In 1976 a pair of three-car sets of inner suburban units await the evening peak and a journey to Gordon Hill. Broad Street station and the line to Dalston Junction finally closed in 1986, with North London Line services diverted to Stratford.

The former route towards Broad Street stayed trackless until most of the line was reopened in 2010 as part of the upgrade of the Underground's East London Line and its transfer to Network Rail, with services being operated by a new franchise – London Overground. These major works included a new formation and station at Shoreditch plus the construction of some intermediate stations. One of these was Hoxton, photographed on 30 April 2010 as northbound unit 378 145 arrives. Meanwhile, the city's skyline is continuing to evolve upwards.

After the demise of trains to Broad Street, the North Woolwich to Richmond service was provided by former Southern Region 2EPB units (Class 416). In September 1988 6320 arrives at Highbury & Islington heading for North Woolwich. Note that bars had been fitted over the opening windows to prevent decapitation approaching Hampstead Tunnel. The 2EPB sets were later replaced by dual-voltage 313 units.

The North London Line has long been a major freight artery and remains so today. On 19 March 2009 Freightliner's 66 538 heads eastwards through Highbury & Islington's back platform (normally used only during disruption) on the bidirectional single line dedicated to non-passenger trains. However, the area has since been completely remodelled to cater for terminating trains from the East London Line.

Commencing May 2000, Anglia Railways introduced an innovative new service from East Anglia to Basingstoke, using the North London Line to gain access to the Southern Region. Class 170 DMUs were used on these duties, but the infrequency and the roundabout route meant that the trains were little used. Just before the demise of such workings, in summer 2002, 170 204 was photographed passing Camden Road East Junction, heading for Hampshire.

Camden Road station, reduced to just two tracks, could be considered to be a bit of a bottleneck, with frequent freight mixing with the regular interval passenger service. Both AC and DC electrification systems are visible in this picture of Yeoman 59 004 *Paul A Hammond* on a westbound empty aggregate train passing through the station in mid-2000. The locomotive, one of the first to be bought by a UK private operator, had been new fifteen years earlier.

Camden Road Junction signal box was at the west end of the passenger station and is seen to good effect on a sunny day in spring 2000. Silverlink liveried unit 313 134, originally built for GN inner suburban services, comes off the line from Gospel Oak, heading for North Woolwich. Silverlink, owned by National Express, ran the North London Line services from 1997 until 2007, when London Overground took over.

At this point it is convenient to take a look at another of London's orbital routes, that from Barking to Gospel Oak. On December 1993 Network Southeast Class 117 DMU set No. L703 was photographed departing from Barking station. Until 1981, this service ran to Kentish Town, where it would have connected with services into St Pancras.

Today the Barking to Gospel Oak line has been electrified and the passenger service is in the hands of modern EMUs operated by London Overground. One of them, numbered 710 269, a four-car set, calls at Woodgrange Park on 19 July 2019. At the time of writing, an extension of the line is under construction to serve Barking Riverside. (Hugh Llewelyn)

South Tottenham station, on the Barking to Gospel Oak line, also has connections to both of the former Great Eastern Railway's Lea Valley routes. On 2 November 2010, the station saw the unusual sight of 87 002 *Royal Sovereign*, owned by the AC Locomotive Group, in charge of a Network Rail test train. The train, having just come from Tottenham South Junction, will take the curve to Seven Sisters.

Once first generation DMUs had been withdrawn from the Barking to Gospel Oak line, Class 150 units were drafted in, but were soon replaced by more modern 'Turbostars'. One of them, two-car set No. 172 006, in London Overground colours, sits in the terminating platform at Gospel Oak on 2 November 2010. As we have already seen, modern Class 710 units have now taken over the electrified service.

Towards the north end of the West London Line is North Pole Junction that, until recently, gave access to the Eurostar depot. On 6 July 2009 EWS loco 92 031 *The Institute of Logistics and Transport* was photographed on an empty steel working. It is passing the connections to the Eurostar facility, already out of use by then, having been replaced by the new Temple Mills depot.

Another view at North Pole Junction, on 4 September 2009, as steam locomotive 60163 *Tornado* brings up the rear of the empties of 'The Winton Train'. This was a private passenger service, from Prague to Liverpool Street, London, commemorating the efforts of Sir Nicholas Winton to get a large group of Czechoslovakian children (mainly of Jewish origin) from Prague to London in 1939. The locomotive itself is much younger, having only been completed in 2008.

In early 1971 we see diesel locomotive D5186 shunting passenger stock at Kensington Olympia, the most important station on the West London Line, though at the time it was only served by the Clapham Junction shuttle, Motorail services and special workings for the adjacent Olympia Exhibition Hall. D5186 had been built at BR's Derby Works in 1963 and moved to duties in the capital in 1969. It was later repainted into BR corporate blue and renumbered as 25 036, with withdrawal coming in 1986. (Tony Martens)

In the 1970s Kensington Olympia was controlled by semaphore signalling, with LNWR style boxes at either end of the station. Kensington North Main signal box is illustrated here in this 1978 photograph along with a mixture of upper and lower quadrant signals. The station area has since been very much simplified and signalling is in the hands of Victoria power box that is located at Clapham Junction.

The fortunes of the West London Line have certainly taken several turns for the better. The line is now electrified as part of the London Overground network, while Southern also runs a regular service over the line to Milton Keynes. New stations have been opened. These are at Shepherds Bush and Imperial Wharf , while new platforms on the WLL have been built to provide interchange with the District Line at West Brompton. Around a year after the reopening, Silverlink EMU 313 134 calls on a southbound working in summer 2000.

Passenger workings on the North London Line reach their terminus at Richmond, connecting with South West Trains and London Underground. For some time a spare DMU was kept here in case it was needed on the Gospel Oak-Barking service. On 19 May 2006 Silverlink liveried 'Sprinter' set 150 030, named *Bedford-Bletchley 150* was photographed here.

London Underground

The line between Finsbury Park on the former Great Northern Railway and Moorgate was built to 'tube' standards, but with large enough diameter tunnels to allow the passage of normal-sized trains from the national network. By the early 1970s, the service along the line, now in the hands of London Transport, was just a shuttle between Drayton Park and Moorgate. In 1971, a short set of 1938 'tube' stock is seen on arrival into daylight at its northern terminus, with the depot alongside. In 1976, the line passed into the hands of British Rail.

Though they were named the '1938 Stock', London Transport's red-liveried tube trains were built in Birmingham from 1938, with the last deliveries being in 1953. The Bakerloo Line was the last to see these trains in front-line service, though they were also used on other lines. In the summer of 1978 a service pulls into the platforms at Queens Park, prior to setting out on a journey to Elephant & Castle. The 1938 sets lasted until 1988 on Underground metals, but some were sold for further service on the Isle of Wight.

London Transport's 1959 tube stock was constructed in Birmingham for the Piccadilly Line. It was used on such duties until the mid-1970s, when it was moved to both the Northern and Bakerloo lines. On 1971, a typical set is seen at Acton Town, having just terminated after a trip through central London.

Although it was intended to be a big batch, the 1960 tube stock consisted of only twelve driving motor cars. Earlier trailer carriages were inserted to form four-car sets. They were used on semi-rural Central Line services in East London and Essex, including the prototype automatic operation as a precursor to the introduction of such on the new Victoria Line. This took in the Woodford to Hainault service. It reverted to normal manual operating practices in 1986, when this photograph of a set reduced to a three-car formation was taken at Hainault.

The Central Line started to receive new trains in 1993, built at Derby. Known as the '1992 Stock', problems were later encountered, including a traction motor becoming detached causing a derailment. The units are fitted with automatic working, with the driver normally just operating the doors manually. In early 1995, one of the sets is seen northbound at Newbury Park.

The newest route on the London Underground network is the Jubilee Line, taking over the Stanmore branch from the Bakerloo and running through Central London to Canary Wharf and Stratford. New trains, known as the '1983 Stock', were introduced, but proved very unreliable. They were used on the initial Stanmore to Charing Cross service, and on such a duty a set is seen in 1986, having terminated at Wembley Park. '1996 Stock' (see Page 31) has now replaced these units, which were sent for scrap.

Sometime around 1986, a set of 1959 tube stock departs Totteridge and Whetstone on the Northern Line, heading for the terminus at High Barnet. This line was built as a branch of the Great Northern Railway and passed to the LNER in 1923. Northern Line services commenced in 1940, with British Railways' freight ceasing as late as 1962.

The 1959 Stock, seen in the previous picture, was later replaced by new 1995 Stock, built by GEC Alstom in Birmingham, a situation that still applies at the time of writing. On a sunny spring day in 2003, a southbound set arrives at Hendon Central on the Edgware branch.

London Transport's Victoria Line was opened in stages from 1968 to 1971, operated by fully automatic trains of 1967 Stock trains. One of these is seen arriving at Kings Cross/St Pancras at an ungodly hour of the morning *c*. 1977, as the author was en route to his employment at Victoria.

With the extension of the Jubilee Line from Charing Cross, through Docklands, to Stratford, new 1996 Stock was received and a set was photographed at its Stratford terminus in 1999.

We now move away from the deep-level 'tube' lines to look at London Transport's other railways, which operate at sub-surface in the centre, but out in the open air elsewhere. One of these is the District Line, which runs from Upminster in the east to three termini to the west of London. On the Richmond branch, partly shared with British Rail in 1974, a set of 'R' stock (built in the 1950s) is under the control of semaphore signals as it makes its stop at Gunnersbury.

For the Metropolitan Line, running out into rural Buckinghamshire, London Transport acquired the 'A' Stock, featuring comfortable 3&2 seating. Built by Cravens of Sheffield, a typical set arrives at Harrow-on-the-Hill on a working bound for Aldgate in October 1996. These units lasted until 2012 when they were replaced by new 'S' Stock, which now handle all sub-surface duties.

London Transport's 'C' Stock entered service from 1970 and consisted of two batches (C69 and C77), to be used mainly on the Circle and Hammersmith & City Lines. Originally delivered in all-silver livery, later refurbishment saw the units receive a few splashes of colour as seen applied to this set at Earls Court station in the summer of 1993. These trains saw plenty of service until final withdrawal in 2014.

For the District Line, London Transport ordered seventy-five sets of 'D' stock, each consisting of six cars. A typical set, led by car 7122, is seen arriving on a Richmond service at Kew Gardens on 12 April 2006. Withdrawal of these units came in 2016 and 2017, with the introduction of the new 'S' Stock. It was felt in the railway industry that there was life left in these relatively new trains and Vivarail has converted several for use on rural lines, with more planned, in both diesel and electric operation.

The new 'S' Stock is now in use on all sub-surface lines of London Underground. Here a set forms a Richmond to Upminster service calling at the former LSWR station of Kew Gardens, taken on 23 April 2019.

Occasionally there are unusual workings over London Underground metals. Perhaps one of the rarest is that of former BR Park Royal two-car DMU, numbers RDB975089 and 975090, in use as a track recording train. It is seen in the platforms of Hammersmith (H&C) station on 5 December 1984. (From an original slide in author's collection, photographer unknown).

When engineering work requires the isolation of London Underground's traction current, 'tube'-sized battery locomotives are employed. One of thirteen built by Metro-Cammell in the mid-1960s, No. 21 is seen at Acton Works during the open day in August 1983. (Tony Martens)

One of the sets used on the Hainault Loop of the Central Line (see Page 28) was later converted to become a track recording train. As such, it was photographed as it headed south through Harrow-on-the-Hill, on the Metropolitan Line, on 29 February 2012.

Docklands Light Railway

Fully automated since opening in 1987, the Docklands Light Railway (DLR) was built to assist in the redevelopment of the former London Docks, centered on what is now Canary Wharf. The initial system consisted of two lines, one from Tower Gateway and the other from Stratford. Both terminated by the Thames at Island Gardens. It is here, in the autumn of the opening year, that we see set No. 10 arriving. One of eleven such units, they were built in Germany and have since returned to their home country, where they operate as conventional trams in Essen.

Since that 1987 opening, the DLR has expanded in all directions, including lines to Bank, Woolwich Arsenal, Beckton and Lewisham. New trains have been purchased; with more on order and train length has increased. A double set of these, built by Bombardier, was photographed arriving at Pudding Mill Lane, alongside the GER main line, on 21 August 2009.

Great Northern Lines

It would be amiss of the author if a picture of one of the famous 'Deltic' locomotives was not included in this section. Here is 9003 *Meld* in platform 7 at Kings Cross in 1971. It is awaiting departure with 1S17, which is believed to be the 09:00 to Edinburgh. Entering service in 1961, it was renumbered 55 003 in 1974 and withdrawn in 1980. The following year it succumbed to the breaker's torch at Doncaster Works.

Bringing in the empty stock for 1S17 is Brush type 2 No. 5601, passing the signal box as it arrives at Kings Cross. The train consists of brand new Mark 2D air-conditioned stock. 5601, new as D5601 in 1960, spent most of its early life on the GN suburban network, until, renumbered 31 180, it was transferred to Immingham in 1974. Withdrawal came in 1995 but it was not scrapped until 2003.

Originally built for Lea Valley services out of Liverpool Street, the Class 125 suburban DMU sets were transferred to the GN in the late 1960s. In 1971, one of them was photographed on arrival in Kings Cross station. The platforms shown here, along with the 'Hotel Curve' from the Moorgate line, have now vanished. The electrification of the inner suburban services in 1977 saw the demise of these units.

Alongside the 'throat' of Kings Cross station was, until 1979, a diesel locomotive servicing/ fuelling point, which could easily be viewed from the end of platform 8. Sometime around 1976, a trio of Class 31 locos, including 31 183 and 31 408, occupies it.

After initially being introduced on former Great Western metals, British Rail commenced operation of High Speed Trains (HST) on the East Coast Main Line out of Kings Cross in 1978. Each train consisted of a Class 43 power car at either end. Seen on arrival at Kings Cross in January 1984 is No. 43 045, in its original livery and carrying the name *The Grammar School Doncaster AD 1350.*

Upon privatisation the Great Northern suburban services were awarded to National Express, trading as West Anglia Great Northern. First Group took over the GN routes, plus the Thameslink services, in 2006. On the fourth day of April in that year, the striking new livery was introduced and is seen here applied to unit 365 505 in platform 10 at Kings Cross. This set had originally started life on the Southern Region, operating in DC mode, but later transferred to the GN with 25kv overhead supply.

Hull Trains was formed to run 'open-access' passenger services to Hull from London Kings Cross. Services started in 2000, using Class 170 DMUs, which were replaced by Class 222 'Pioneer' sets, one of which is seen in Kings Cross station on arrival in the evening of 27 July 2008. At that time, control of Hull Trains had passed to First Group (The '*F*' symbol can just be seen). Since then, Class 180 units were employed, now displaced by 802 'Paragon' sets.

No, this is not Platform 9¾ at Kings Cross, but the 'Hogwarts Express' is in one of the more conventionally numbered platforms. In its special maroon livery, preserved 5972 *Olten Hall* was found there during the evening of 25 May 2010.

Virgin Trains East Coast (a joint venture between Stagecoach and Virgin) gained the franchise to run the InterCity services out of Kings Cross, starting on 1 March 2015. Rolling stock consisted of Class 91 locos with Mark V coaches, plus a good number of HST diesel sets. One of these, with power car 43 257 at the south end, is seen in platform 0 (opened in 2010) at Kings Cross on 21 January 2016.

Meaning 'east' in Japanese, 'Azuma' was the name given to the new Hitachi Class 800 units to be used by Virgin Trains East Coast. On 18 March 2013 a brand new set is seen in platform 8 at Kings Cross, prior to setting out on a test run. These impressive trains are now in full service, but run by LNER, the government-owned 'operator of last resort', which took over on 23 June 2018.

In 1976 British Rail took over the former Great Northern & City branch to Moorgate, using dual-voltage Class 313 EMUs. These operated on third rail DC traction from Drayton Park southwards. Initially, a shuttle service ran between Drayton Park and Moorgate and, sometime in 1976, unit 313 013 is seen on arrival in daylight.

Away from the confines of the Moorgate branch, the 313 units operated using power from the 25kv overhead system. After initial teething problems these three-car trains settled down to a long life on the GN section. In First Capital Connect livery, 313 025 was photographed on an up Hertford service at Palmers Green on 17 August 2013. All these sets on the GN were withdrawn in 2019 to be replaced by new Class 717 six-car units. At the time of writing, some 313 EMUs are still in service elsewhere.

For engineering duties between Drayton Park and Moorgate British Rail converted some former Class 501 power cars into locomotives, operating using the third rail or battery power. When not in use, these were kept at the main EMU depot on the GN section at Hornsey. No. 97 704 was photographed around the rear of that location in mid-1992.

As a major depot, Hornsey boasted a wheel lathe and this was used on a regular basis by units from other lines, such as this NSE liveried Thameslink EMU, 319 036, in mid-1992. Hornsey depot has since been expanded and the wheel lathe replaced.

InterCity trains were cleaned and maintained to the north of Hornsey, at Bounds Green depot, visible from Alexandra Palace station. During a visit there in 1992, the unique 89 001 was photographed, out of use, close to the remains of Palace Gates station. The loco was withdrawn soon after, but later re-entered service with GNER (then the operators of the ECML franchise). After a major failure in 2001 it was taken out of service again and is now in preservation.

The Class 317 type of EMU was based on the BR Mark III body shell and the various versions operated on the Midland, Great Northern, Great Eastern and LT&S lines over many years. One of the original ones built to operate out of St Pancras, seen here numbered 317 342, is seen passing New Southgate in First Capital Connect livery colours on 13 September 2010. At the time of writing, these units are nearing the end of their lives.

Prior to BR taking over the Northern City Line, GN services were able to use the 'Widened Lines' between Kings Cross and Moorgate via Farringdon. Sometime around 1975, a set of Class 105 Cravens DMU cars has just left Farringdon and will soon pass under LT's Circle Line as they head back to GN metals. The connection in the foreground was used for stock transfer between the two operators, mainly for the isolated Northern City Line.

British Rail also used loco-hauled non-corridor stock on suburban services, including those to Moorgate. In 1976, 31 188 is seen powering up the grade into Farringdon station. Later in that year, GN services ceased on the 'Widened Lines'. However, services from the Midland Main Line continued and were electrified. Moorgate-bound trains still ran, peak hours only, even after the cross-London Thameslink services were introduced, but ceased in 2009.

Midland Lines

The year 1983 saw the Midland line out of Moorgate and St Pancras to Bedford electrified, but InterCity services to the East Midlands and Yorkshire were still in the hands of BR's Class 45 locomotives. At the time of this photograph, in early 1983, DMUs were operating local routes and one can be seen as 45 118 *The Royal Artilleryman* arrives from the north.

InterCity services out of St Pancras were later taken over by HST sets, which passed to National Express-owned Midland Mainline upon privatisation. In the colours of that franchise, power car 43 076 was photographed at St Pancras, as the station was being transformed into St Pancras International, on 5 April 2008.

Heading north out of St Pancras, the first station is Kentish Town. Until 1981, connections could be made here for the local service to Barking. Ten years earlier a three-car DMU is seen in the station forming such a train. The curve around to the Barking line has since been lifted and trains diverted to Gospel Oak.

With the completion of the first Thameslink project in 1988, the original Bedford to St Pancras Class 317 EMUs were transferred away and replaced by dual-voltage units of Class 319. Numerically the earliest if the batch, 319 001, is arriving at Mill Hill Broadway, in First Capital Connect colours, on 5 August 2011. Variants of the Class 700 EMUs have since taken over.

Out from Euston

London Euston station serves three types of services: the DC Lines stopping trains to Watford Junction, AC outer suburban and InterCity expresses to the West Midlands and the North. The southern section of the West Coast Main Line had been electrified in 1965 and Euston station modernised. In 1971, one of the Doncaster-built electric locomotives, No. E3081, awaits it next duty at country end of Euston station. This loco was later renumbered 85 026 and lasted until it was scrapped in 1993.

Of the 1960s electric locomotives built for the WCML the type known as AL6 was undoubtedly the most successful. Under the TOPS renumbering of the early 1970s, they became Class 86 and one of the batch, 86 258, is seen propelling the empty stock of the 'Manchester Pullman' into Euston station in 1979. This service, using special Mark 2 carriages, ceased operating in 1985. 86 258 lasted a few years longer, but has since been scrapped. A few of its sisters remain in service at the time of writing.

AC electric locomotive 82 005 was one of a batch of only ten built in the early 1960s by AEI. Originally numbered E3051, it was latterly used to take empty coaching stock between depots and termini. Seen on the stops at Euston in the summer of 1983, it was withdrawn four years later and was scrapped in Booth's yard, Rotherham.

Network Rail's 'New Measurement Train', formed of HST power cars and various converted passenger carriages, tours the national network seeking out track faults as it travels at line speed. On 2 May 2006 it was photographed in Euston station, having just arrived.

Initially designated as AM10 units, the London Midland Region received fifty four-car EMUs for London outer suburban services and other duties around the West Midlands. These were later known as Class 310 and one is seen, numbered 061, in Euston station, still in all-over blue, in 1978.

As well as the North London Line, the so-called 'DC Lines' stopping service from Euston to Watford Junction was the preserve of BR's Class 501 three-car EMUs. Heading north in 1978 is a typical off-peak working, calling at Harlesden station. In the mid-1980s, these services were taken over by Class 313 units, which later gave way to more modern sets of Class 378 stock run by London Overground.

One of the first locomotives to be delivered to BR for the WCML electrification, AL1/Class 81 No. E3005, is seen in the yards at Willesden in 1974. Behind is the Freightliner terminal, since closed, while forming the most prominent backdrop are the cooling towers of Acton Lane Power Station. After thirty years service E3005, renumbered 81 004, was withdrawn in 1990.

Acton Lane Power Station was rail served and, until rail traffic ceased in 1981, operated its own steam locomotives. One of them, ED5, a Barclay 0-4-0ST named *Little Barford*, is seen at work here. The photograph was actually taken in 1967, though nothing changed into the 1970s. The power station ceased operations totally in 1983. (Alan James)

Newly renumbered in 1974, AL6 electric locomotive 86 203 is seen departing from the yards at Harlesden with a test train. This was one of three that were converted to become test-beds for the development of the Class 87. New as E3143, it later became 86 103 and passed into the hands of Virgin Trains and withdrawn in 1995.

Seen from the low-level platforms at Willesden Junction station, EWS liveried 350HP shunter 08 783 passes by on the connection up to the North London Line, heading east towards Kensal Rise in October 2002. Built in 1960, this shunter is no longer in service.

On the West Coast Main Line, Freightliner 70 019 pilots 66 672 with a northbound container train on 20 February 2015. They are passing South Kenton station on the DC Lines, which are also used by London Underground's Bakerloo Line services to Harrow & Wealdstone.

No look at the WCML would be complete without a view of one of the Class 390 'Pendolino' sets, which feature tilt technology. An up service is seen on an up Virgin Trains service speeding through Harrow & Wealdstone on 4 April 2006, only a few years after entering service. The WCML franchise has since passed to Avanti West Coast (First Group and Trenitalia) and the red Virgin colours have disappeared.

Marylebone Services

The Great Central Railway's London terminus at Marylebone opened in the last year of the nineteenth century. The station's main line services finished in 1966, leaving only the suburban routes towards Aylesbury and High Wycombe. It was threatened with closure in the 1980s, but fortunately reprieved by Network SouthEast. Here is the exterior of the station in 1982, looking very much like a provincial town facility.

Inside Marylebone station in mid-1987, a four-car Class 115 DMU awaits departure for High Wycombe. This type of DMU was later replaced by Class 165 'Turbo' sets.

In the 1980s Marylebone became well used to handling steam excursions. On 11 July 1987, rebuilt 'Merchant Navy' 35028 *Clan Line* is being prepared for departure with Crookham Travel's 'Half Century Pullman' destined for Kidderminster and the Severn Valley Railway. 35028 worked as far as Knowle & Dorridge, where it was replaced by a diesel.

Heading out of Marylebone, the line towards High Wycombe diverges from the Aylesbury route at Neasden Junction, passes Wembley Stadium and joins the line from Paddington at Northolt Junction. Here, in the late 1980s, semaphore signalling still controlled movements, as a Class 50 has the road for the GW line. (From an original slide in the author's collection, photographer unknown).

The outermost station in Greater London on the High Wycombe route is West Ruislip, where a physical connection is made with London Underground's Central Line. This can be seen on the left of this photograph, though little used at the time, on 5 August 2011. Chiltern Railways' 165 004 heads out on the down line.

Under the management of the Chiltern Railways franchise, great improvements have been made to services out of Marylebone. Trains now run direct to Oxford (via a new curve at Bicester) and to Birmingham. Some of the latter are of push-pull formation, using Direct Rail Services Class 68 locomotives built in Spain. Some of these are painted in Chiltern Railways' colours, but 68 009 *Titan* wears DRS blue at Marylebone on 12 May 2016.

Former GWR Lines

Brush type 4 D1934 was built in 1966 and retained its BR green colours until 1978. It was photographed as 47 256 at Paddington in 1976 awaiting the road as a 'light engine' movement, probably to Old Oak Common. This loco remained on the Western Region until 1988 and was in service until final withdrawal in 2001.

A total of seventy-four Class 52 diesel hydraulic locomotives were built for Western Region main line duties, with deliveries being in the early 1960s. Being non-standard, they did not find favour with BR's higher authorities and the first withdrawals began in 1973. Never receiving TOPS numbers, allegedly due to cast number plates, D1030 *Western Musketeer* is seen in Paddington station, oozing fumes and steam, in 1976. D1030 was scrapped soon after the photograph was taken.

The Great Western main line was the first InterCity route to receive Class 253 high speed trains, entering full service in 1976. In that year set 253 001 (they were considered by BR to be DMUs when first introduced) awaits departure at Paddington for Bristol. Power car No. 43 002 is the leading vehicle. It was lucky enough to enter preservation and can usually be found at York's National Railway Museum.

Built by Pressed Steel, the Class 117 DMUs were introduced onto Paddington suburban services in the early 1960s. In the spring of 1983 a three-car set, numbered L410, arrives at the London terminus, running alongside London Underground's Hammersmith & City Line.

In spring 1983 BR was still running dedicated mail and parcels services and an unusual working was captured on film as it entered Paddington station. Leading is Gloucester RCW built parcels DMU W55992, while behind is a single Class 121 DMU car.

In 1986 the Paddington suburban services, as well as routes to Oxford, Newbury and beyond, became part of Network SouthEast. A striking new livery was introduced and the first locomotive to wear these colours was 50 023 *Howe*. Here it is, just after receiving its new paintwork in 1986, at Paddington station. The Class 50 locomotives were built for WCML duties north of Preston, but electrification saw them redeployed to the Western Region. 50 023, originally numbered D423, was scrapped at Barrow Hill in 2004.

Construction of the Heathrow Airport branch of the National Rail system began in 1993. Opened in 1998, it is a 2-mile line, leaving the GW main line west of Hayes & Harlington by means of a 'flying junction'. The Paddington to the airport route was electrified as a consequence. A total of fourteen Class 332 EMU sets were built in Spain for the Heathrow Express service. In the first year of operation, four-car unit 332 004 is seen in Paddington station. The future of these units is, at the time of writing, uncertain, as it is expected that Class 387 'Electrostars' will operate the service.

ABB at York built the 165 and 166 classes of DMU for Paddington and Marylebone services in the early 1990s. The Class 166 versions featured air conditioning and were intended for longer distance services such as those to Oxford and beyond. In common with all rolling stock that passed to Great Western (a First Group company), these units were painted into the dark green livery and one of the first to receive it was 166 212, seen at Paddington on 25 April 2016.

The 'Electrostar' family of EMUs are now familiar sights out of several London termini, but perhaps the most striking are those of GWR on services out of Paddington. Painted in all-over dark green, 387 131 slows as it passes Royal Oak LUL station and approaches its destination on 23 April 2019.

The Hitachi-built Class 800 units are now in full front-line service on GWR InterCity services out of Paddington. Here, five-car set 800 026 is seen using electrical power as it accelerates out of Paddington on 23 April 2019.

A memorable day in 1981 as the last steam locomotive built for British Railways, 9F 2-10-0 No 92220, happily in preservation, powers along the Great Western main line on 20 June. It was photographed near Westbourne Park, just a mile or so out of Paddington. (Tony Martens)

The main depot for servicing locomotives and multiple units on the route out of Paddington was at Old Oak Common. The main repair shops, always known as 'The Factory', are seen in this photograph of preserved diesel hydraulic locomotives D821 *Greyhound* and D1015 *Western Champion*. This pair was in attendance for one of the open days held here in the 1990s. Enormous changes are in progress in this area, with GWR taking over the redundant Eurostar depot and an interchange station being built for both the Elizabeth Line and HS2.

Another photograph taken at an open day in Old Oak Common locomotive yard sees 47 234 in Railfreight Distribution livery. Starting life in 1962 as D1911, it was later rebuilt as 57 315, operating for West Coast Railways.

Not far west of Old Oak Common is Acton Yard, one of London's busiest freight locations. The east end exit from the sidings is easily viewed from Acton Main Line station, from where, on 5 August 2011, DB liveried 59 206 was photographed. This locomotive had been delivered in 1995 to National Power for Yorkshire coal services and passed to EWS in 1998, who transferred it to Southern England for heavy aggregate duties.

Further out of London is Ealing Broadway, where interchange can be made with LUL's District and Central lines. One of the latter's 1959 sets can be seen as Class 117 DMU set L401 arrives in the station on the down relief line, forming a service to Reading. The unit is newly painted in NSE colours, dating the photograph to *c.* 1989. (From an original transparency in the author's collection, photographer unknown)

The Great Western Railway did not have 'slow lines'. When two lines became congested and new ones built, they were always known as 'relief lines'. Out of Paddington, these were used for suburban passenger trains and, even today, a considerable amount of freight. Here, on 12 February 2015, Freightliner's 66 523 heads a cement train through Ealing Broadway on the up relief line.

Southall, on the GW main line, was once an important place, being the junction with the Brentford branch and the location of a large motive power depot. Part of the branch is still in use for freight, while the loco shed is now in private hands and used to maintain steam locos and other 'heritage' items. Passing through Southall station in 1989, on a 'light engine' working along the down relief, is 59 002 *Yeoman Enterprise*. Painted in Yeoman's colours, this locomotive is normally to be found hauling stone trains to and from the Mendip Hills. At the time of writing, Southall station is receiving a major upgrade as part of the Crossrail project.

The branch to Heathrow Airport leaves the main line to the west of Hayes & Harlington station. Departing from that station on its way to Paddington is Heathrow Connect unit 360 201 on a stopping service on 10 August 2007. A total of five of these units were delivered as four-car sets, which later gained an extra car each. In 2018, Heathrow Connect passed to TfL Rail and the Class 360 units were withdrawn as non-standard and placed into storage.

At what is now close to the site of Heathrow Junction, west of Hayes & Harlington, Network SouthEast liveried 50 024 *Vanguard* leads a down service along the fast line, *c.* 1988. New in 1968 for West Coast Main Line services north of Crewe, it was later transferred to the Western Region and was scrapped at Old Oak Common in 1991.

Meanwhile, back at Paddington, sometime around 1978, we see 31 413 just arrived with empty coaching stock in platform 1. Judging by the locomotive's condition, it had recently been on Royal Train duties, probably having hauled Her Majesty to Tattenham Corner on Derby Day. When new in 1961, this locomotive was delivered to Sheffield Darnall depot and continued in use in the Yorkshire area until the early 1970s. It was finally withdrawn in 1997.

Another loco that had been used to bring empty coaching stock into Paddington, EW&S 37 109, has followed an enthusiasts' special to the end of the platform and now awaits the signal out of the station in the spring of 1997. New in 1963 as D6809, it had been employed on the Eastern Region in its earlier years and is still operational today, on the East Lancashire Railway.

In 1985 Class 117 DMU set B430 (consisting of car numbers 51410, 59520 and 51368) was repainted into GWR livery to help celebrate 'GWR 150'. Here it is, in Paddington station, forming a semi-fast service to Didcot in May 1986. (Tony Martens)

Before leaving the Western Region, we take a look at the former Great Western line from Acton to Northolt and the junction with the route from Marylebone near South Ruislip. At Park Royal, the Guinness Brewery manufactured its products for much of mainland Great Britain. Having opened in 1936, the business was rail connected and two locomotives were delivered in the late 1940s from F. Hibberd & Co., just down the road in Park Royal. Here we see *Carpenter* (Works No. 3270) resting between duties in the brewery sidings. Sister loco *Walrus* is preserved at Quainton Road. The Hibberd locos were later replaced by a hired-in BR Class 08. The brewery closed in 2005, so the draught Guinness served in the UK today is brewed in Ireland.

In 1903, the Great Western Railway opened a 2.5-mile-long railway between West Ealing on the main line and Greenford on the Acton to Northolt route. A half-hourly shuttle service operates between Ealing and Greenford, where there is a bay sandwiched between the two Central Line Underground platforms. Sometime around 1976, a single car Class 121 DMU (55027 – L127) is ready to depart with an evening working to Ealing Broadway. A new platform was constructed at West Ealing in 2017 and the shuttle now terminates there.

Southern Region
(South Western Division)

Opened in 1898 and operated by the London & South Western Railway, the Waterloo & City Line is a deep-level tube line connecting Waterloo main line with Bank station in the heart of the City of London. On 1 April 1994 the line was transferred to London Underground, having already been equipped with new rolling stock a year earlier. Almost identical to the trains used on the Central Line, one of the sets, numbered 482 501, is seen at Bank station in November 1993.

Until Waterloo station underwent major changes with the building of the Eurostar terminal, the only rail access to the Waterloo & City Line was via this lift built by Armstrong Whitworth. It was connected to the sidings situated on the north side of the station and is seen here in the late 1970s. Note the trap points stopping unintended movements onto the lift. A serious accident did occur here in 1948 with a class M7 0-4-4T falling down the shaft.

Within Waterloo station sometime around 1977, two types of suburban EMUs are seen side by side. On the left, in platform 5, is 4SUB unit 4624, just arrived, while 2EPB set 5936 is in platform 4. The black triangle is there to advise station staff that the guard's compartment is at that end of the two-car unit. A close look will reveal the differences between the types of EMUs. The 4SUB has only air braking and the use of a tail lamp is necessary, while a screw coupler is used to attach it to another set. Indicator blinds on the EPB set double as a tail lamp, a buckeye coupling is fitted and twenty-seven pin jumpers ensure continuity of the electro-pneumatic braking system.

Back in 1974 shunting duties at Waterloo justified the use of a 350hp diesel shunter as the 'station pilot'. Recently numbered as 08 642, this locomotive had been new in 1959 as D3809, when it was allocated to the Western Region. It was transferred to the Southern in 1971 and lasted until withdrawn in 2006.

Seen in a short bay platform at Waterloo station is 33 112, one of the push-pull fitted 'Crompton' mixed traffic diesels built by the Birmingham Railway Carriage & Wagon Company. Delivered in 1960 as D6529, it was initially allocated to Hither Green, but later transferred to the South Western. The photograph was taken *c.* 1978. 33 112 was later named *Templecombe* and as such survived until withdrawal in 1988.

In the 1990s it became fairly common to find Class 37 locomotives operating on London's Southern Region lines, but to find one at Waterloo was relatively rare. Engineering work in the spring of 1995 found 37 185, named *Lea & Perrins*, in the station. Built in 1963, it had worked most of its life in South Wales, but in its later years was allocated to the Glasgow, Yorkshire and East Midland areas. It was withdrawn in 1999, but not cut up until 2006.

Waterloo station underwent a major change in the early 1990s. Platforms 20 and 21, on the 'Windsor Side', were demolished to make way for the new five-platform Eurostar terminal. This was opened for regular services on 14 November 1994, with through trains to Paris and Brussels. A year or so after opening, half set No. 3005 is seen at the buffer stop end of platform 23, soon to depart for the Continent. With the opening of the full length of the Channel Tunnel Rail Link in 2007, Eurostar services were diverted to St Pancras. That part of the station has since been reallocated to domestic services.

Construction of the 4CEP EMUs began in 1956, mainly for the Kent Coast electrification. Twenty-two of the four-car units were designated as 4BEPs (later Class 410) as each contained a buffet car. During the refurbishment programme of the late 1970s/early 1980s, several were converted to conventional 4CEP units, but the few rebuilt 4BEPs were transferred to the South Western Division. Seen in full NSE colours, at Waterloo, in the spring of 1996 is unit 2303. South West Trains withdrew the last 4BEP as late as 2005.

Originally built by BREL Derby Works as conventional Class 158 DMUs, the ones for use on the BR's South Western Division services from Waterloo to Salisbury and Exeter were modified at Rosyth Dockyard to become NSE Class 159. At privatisation, these passed to South West Trains. Seen in that livery at Waterloo on 17 April 2008 is three-car set 159 009.

Steam trains are not unknown at Waterloo. On 14 December 2006, preserved 'Black 5' 45231 was found in the station ready to haul 'The Cathedrals Express' down to Sherborne in Dorset, where many participants attended a carol concert at the abbey.

Heading out of London on a semi-fast towards Weymouth, 4CIG (Class 421) EMU 1887 in NSE colours passes through Vauxhall station in October 1999. These units, constructed at York Works, were mainly intended for Central Division duties, but a number, built from 1970 to 1974, were allocated to the South Western.

South West Trains, after initially using Stagecoach stripes, later applied this smart red livery to its suburban EMUs. On 23 April 2019, two-car 456 018 trails a Class 455 unit on its way towards Waterloo as it passes Queenstown Road, Battersea. Another product of York, the Class 456 was constructed in 1990/1 for Central Division services. They were transferred from Southern to South West Trains in 2013, after refurbishment.

One island platform, on the so-called 'Windsor Lines', is sufficient to provide the needs of Queenstown Road, Battersea station. It is 23 April 2019 and South Western Railway DMU 159 013 passes on the down fast. South Western Railway, a joint venture between First Group and MTR (of Hong Kong), took over the franchise from South West Trains in 2017. The new, rather monochrome, livery is well illustrated here.

The Class 442 'Wessex Electric' five-car EMUs were introduced in 1988 to coincide with the Bournemouth to Weymouth third rail electrification. The units were delivered in NSE colours and set No. 2419 (shown here) still retains that livery, albeit with 'SWT' branding. Coupled to a sister unit, the ten-car train was photographed leaving the yard at Clapham Junction in 1988. Following a period of storage, the 442 sets were dedicated to Gatwick Express duties, but are now back on former LSWR metals with South Western Railway.

Regular local passenger services over the West London Line ceased during the Second World War, but an unadvertised peak hour Clapham Junction to Kensington Olympia shuttle was retained to cater for workers at the Post Office Savings Bank HQ. Seen at Clapham Junction, *c.* 1971, on such a working is 'Crompton' No. 6513, later to become 33 102. It was converted for push-pull operation in 1967. Today it is in preservation and operates on the Churnet Valley Railway in Staffordshire.

The initial small batch of Class 73 electro-diesel locomotives were built by BR's Eastleigh Works, but the later 73/1 variants were constructed at Vulcan Foundry, Newton-le-Willows. One of them, 73 110, was found on an officers' special at Clapham Junction sometime around 1975. New in 1966, this loco has had a long life, having entered preservation following withdrawal, though it was later sold to GBRf and last reported as stored at Eastleigh.

By 1981, when this photograph was taken, the 4SUB units were on their last legs. Here we have No. 4660 leading a similar set and calling at Clapham Junction on an up service from Hampton Court.

For South Western Division suburban duties, a large batch of Class 508 EMUs were built at York Works. Outwardly similar to the 313 units, the 508s were capable only of operating on third rail DC lines. On the same occasion as the upper picture, 508 041 calls at Clapham Junction on a Kingston to Waterloo service. This class was later transferred to Merseyside and replaced in the south by units of Class 455. At the time of writing, Merseyrail is receiving new EMUs to replace the 508s and similar 507s.

A sunny 1 June 2017 sees South West Trains EMU 458 528 arriving at Clapham Junction on a down service on the 'Windsor' side of the station. Thirty of these units were built by Alstom and are reputed to be the first new fleet to be delivered to a privatised operator. They were intended for semi-fast and outer suburban duties, but often appeared on main line services too.

The principal depot for the South Western Division's suburban fleet was at Wimbledon and here is a view of part of that facility, *c*. 1971. Poking a couple of carriages outside one of the sheds is an all-over blue 4VEP outer suburban set. Alongside is one of only two 4PEP units, the forerunner of the Class 508 sets. At the time of the photograph, the PEP stock was still undergoing testing. Regular passenger workings did not commence until 1973 and these ceased in 1977, when the units were transferred to BR's Research Department in Derby.

Though Southern Railway passenger services on the East Putney to Wimbledon line ceased in 1941, this bit of railway remained in BR ownership. It was used by empty coaching stock to access part of Wimbledon depot. London Transport's District Line had running powers and was by far the major operator. On this short section, Wimbledon Park station, though served only by LT services, was, in 1971, fully branded as a BR station and boasted a fine ex-LSWR signal box. The East Putney to Wimbledon route was sold to London Underground in 1994, but remains available to South Western Railway for diversions and empty coaching stock, etc.

The Class 444 EMUs were built by Siemens in Austria for South West Trains' front-line duties and were intended to replace the remaining slam-door sets on these works. Maintained at Northam depot, Southampton, these five-car units operate the fast Bournemouth and Weymouth services. On 30 November 2015, 444 024 speeds through Surbiton on it way to the coast.

Southern Region (Central Division)

The 1982 ASLEF rail strike brought some unusual workings into London, including this nine-car Class 119 DMU, with set L572 at the north end. It was photographed in platform 10 of London Victoria and was forming a Brighton service. On the Southern Region, these DMUs, normally running as three-car sets, would be operating the Tonbridge/Gatwick Airport to Reading service via Redhill. It looks as though the litter picking gang are needed!

On 21 February 2008 Class 460 EMU, identified only as '02', sits in the darkness within Victoria station awaiting departure for Gatwick Airport. Delivery of these dedicated eight-car units commenced in 2000, built by Alstom. They replaced the previous Mark II carriages operated in push-pull mode with Class 73 locomotives. After around ten years service, the Class 460 units were withdrawn in favour of refurbished 442 'Wessex Electrics', while the 460s were later converted to 458/5 units for South West Trains. The yellow grids between the rails were installed to work the selective door operations on 377 units, as this was controlled by GPS, which could not penetrate the buildings covering the station.

Here is one of the 'Wessex Electrics' operating with the Go Ahead Group on its Gatwick Express service. 442 417 speeds southwards through Clapham Junction on 21 January 2011. These units did not last long on such duties and had gone by 2017. They have since been refurbished and operate on London to Portsmouth services with South Western Railway.

The BR Class 207 diesel-electric multiple units (DEMUs) were introduced in 1962, mainly for Oxted Line service, with the two routes being non-electrified beyond Sanderstead. Consisting of one power car and two trailers, set No. 1319 arrives at Clapham Junction on an up working from Uckfield on a gloomy spring day in 1979. This particular set, numerically the last, was later renumbered as 207 019 and was scrapped in 1988.

While most of the 4CEP EMUs were allocated to the South Eastern Division, the first batch were used on the former London, Brighton & South Coast Railway territory, particularly on fast services via Horsham. On such a working, heading for London Victoria, No. 7101 calls at Clapham Junction in spring 1979. Being built in 1956, unit 7101 had a different style of interior decoration than the later deliveries, featuring a lot more wooden mouldings.

As well as Victoria, the Central Division used London Bridge as a major terminus, mainly for rush hour traffic to the City of London. Though built by the Southern Railway for its fast Portsmouth services, by the early 1970s these 4COR units were reaching the end of their working lives and were confined to semi-fast duties, including some on the 'Brighton' lines. Here, sometime around 1970/1, we see unit 3139 in platform 9 at London Bridge, as the driver makes his way to his cab.

Perhaps the most unusual locomotive to be seen at London Bridge, London Transport ex-Metropolitan Railway electric locomotive 12 *Sarah Siddons*. It had been retained by London Transport as a brake block testing unit, but 1984 saw it converted to be able to run on the Southern Region's third rail system, prior to working a railtour out of Waterloo on 7 July 1984. A few days before that it had been involved in a test run, hauling a 4EPB unit into London Bridge and was photographed there while running round its load.

As well as its role as a commuter terminus, the terminal platforms at London Bridge saw a considerable amount of mail and newspaper traffic. Here 33 020 waits in platform 13 on a postal service one night in the spring of 1986.

When engineering work meant that the overnight Brighton line newspaper trains were unable to serve Redhill, an additional working from London Bridge utilised a single car motor luggage van (MLV). On this occasion, however, in 1986, a Class 101 set L835 has been found to work the 03.16 to Redhill from platform 8.

Southern's Class 377 'Electrostar' EMUs are to be found on various types of work, including duties in London's suburbs. Here No. 377 143 is seen approaching Sutton from the Carshalton direction on 31 October 2007, probably on a stopping service to Horsham.

The former LB&SCR station at Crystal Palace is a most unusual one. Down trains, directly after emerging from the tunnel, are faced with either a palatial affair to the left, or the sharply curved through platforms on the line towards Norwood Junction. Probably heading for that location, on a cross-London freight, is an unidentified Class 25, *c.* 1975.

The other platforms at Crystal Palace were, in the 1970s, used only during peak hours and for storing empty coaching stock. Seen occupying one of the sidings there, again around 1975, is 4SUB unit 4386.

In contrast to the previous photograph, the former sidings at Crystal Palace have now been replaced by a new island platform for terminating trains from Sydenham and the upgraded London Overground network via the East London Line. Here we see unit 378 232 on 10 March 2011.

A service that is no longer with us is that that used to operate between Victoria and London Bridge via Peckham Rye, though London Overground trains running to and from Clapham Junction have mostly replaced it. In the spring of 1983, a two-car EPB unit is sufficient for the traffic on offer, as set 6303 arrives at Wandsworth Road, having just negotiated the newly laid junction with the line towards Stewarts Lane.

2EPB units were also the mainstay of another South London suburban line, that from West Croydon to Wimbledon via Mitcham Junction. The service started from its own short bay at West Croydon station, which is where we see unit 5753, *c.* 1978. Upon withdrawal of the EPB stock, two-car Class 456 units took over the service.

West Croydon to Wimbledon route was single track for most of its mileage. Between West Croydon and Mitcham Junction trains were able to pass at Waddon Marsh station's island platform. A 2EPB is seen arriving here in 1971, when rail still served the adjacent power station. In its heyday, the line was very busy with freight traffic.

Between Mitcham Junction and Mitcham stations, West Croydon to Wimbledon line was double track. At Mitcham itself, this fine mechanical signal box and a vintage lower quadrant semaphore signal controlled access to the single line northwards, seen in 1971. Mitcham signal box closed in 1982, but the West Croydon to Wimbledon service continued running until 1997, when the line was closed to make way for the new Croydon Tramlink.

One station may have closed in Mitcham, but another one has opened on the Streatham to Sutton line. Situated either side of the busy Eastfields level crossing, the two platforms of Mitcham Eastfields station are seen here, looking towards Mitcham Junction, on 13 June 2008, less than two weeks after being officially opened.

Most of South London's suburban railways see nothing but third rail electric units, so any other workings are always worth a photograph. On 22 August 2008, during the course of his employment, the author was lucky enough to observe Direct Rail Services 37 608 heading through Tulse Hill at the rear of the high-speed track recording train. Another Class 37 is leading the formation.

Until 2008 the Brighton main line was served by a regular working over the cross-country route from the south coast towards Birmingham and Manchester. These had been introduced in the late 1970s by British Rail and continued by Virgin Trains after privatisation. Arriva, trading as Cross Country, later took over the franchise, but the Brighton service was destined to cease. Not long before the service was abolished, we see newly rebranded 'Voyager' DMU set 220 029 calling at East Croydon on its way to the seaside on 1 August 2008.

The motive power of this track testing train is in the form of a Brush type 2 diesel, resplendent in all over yellow. After a long life with British Rail as 31 191, this locomotive was sold to Fragonset, where it was modified to become 31 602 and sold to Network Rail. As such, it is seen in the yard of Southern's Selhurst depot in South London on 18 August 2009.

Selhurst depot has a few sidings dedicated to Southern's small fleet of 'Turbostar' DMUs. These are used on the unelectrified Uckfield line and the 'Marshlink' service from Ashford in Kent into East Sussex. The sets were delivered in both two- and four-car formations, the longer ones being used on the London Bridge to Uckfield route. Four-car 171 805 was photographed at Selhurst between the peaks on 18 August 2009.

Southern Region
(South Eastern Division)

The Class 411 4CEP EMUs were built in the 1950s and '60s for fast services from London to the Kent coast. By the late 1970s, they were looking rather dated, so were heavily rebuilt at Swindon Works. The refurbished ones eventually received NSE colours and two are seen in rather inclement weather at London's Charing Cross terminus in early 1996. All of the class had been withdrawn by 2005.

The first six Class 73 electro-diesel locomotives were built at Eastleigh and entered service in 1962. Here is one of that original batch, No. 73 005 (new as E6005), operating a Christmas special, the 'Kent Hopper'. It is seen passing through London Bridge station heading eastwards in December 1984. After withdrawal, 73 005 entered preservation. It even had a spell on loan to the Severn Valley Railway. It was later sold to GBRf, who had it rebuilt and re-enter service as 73 966, in which guise it often appears on sleeper services in Scotland.

One of London's smallest termini was Holborn Viaduct, from which off-peak suburban services ran along the Catford Loop to Sevenoaks and to Sutton via Tulse Hill. These were supplemented by peak-hour trains to other destinations. Latterly the station consisted of just three platforms, each capable of holding eight-car trains. Here is a view of the station, taken in March 1983, with two platforms occupied by six-carriage EPB stock. Holborn Viaduct closed in 1990, being mostly replaced by the new City Thameslink station.

Before being rebuilt to its present configuration under the Thameslink programme, Blackfriars station consisted of three terminal platforms and two lines passing through en route to Holborn Viaduct. Traffic mainly consisted of a diet of EMUs, so anything different was usually worthy of a photograph. That was certainly the case when former Western Region single-car Class 122 No. 975540 (previously W55016) when it arrived in platform 3 on route learning duties in early 1988.

The present Thameslink routes serve three basic directions heading south after crossing the Thames at Blackfriars. Brighton line services veer off almost immediately, while some head directly south towards Herne Hill. At Loughborough Junction, trains for Sevenoaks take a sharp left turn to reach Denmark Hill, where First Capital Connect 319 385 is seen on 10 January 2013. This train will continue via the Catford Loop to Sevenoaks. The Go Ahead Group now operates all Thameslink services.

Boat trains from the Kent coastal ports were often diverted via the Catford Loop on their way to London Victoria. These often had a motor luggage van (MLV) at the north end of the formation, as seen in this photo. However, the headcode '31' indicates that it is a Dover Priory to Victoria working, booked via Catford. The train, made up of 4CEP units, led by MLV 68005, passes through Bellingham, *c.* 1974.

The Class 465 'Networker' EMUs were introduced in the early 1990s, initially for South Eastern suburban duties. Upon privatisation, these passed to the Connex franchise, which introduced a variation of the former NSE livery. Seen in those colours in Victoria station's platform 3 is 465 006, just arrived from Orpington in autumn 1999. It would be fair to say that the Connex years did not end well, as the company was stripped of its franchise in June 2003.

Just south of the river from Victoria is Stewarts Lane depot, where large numbers of EMUs were maintained, as well as having facilities for locomotives. Seen outside the repair shops in 1982 is 'celebrity' electro-diesel loco 73 142 *Broadlands*. This was a regular performer on the 'Orient Express' Pullmans and other prestigious duties.